The Best of Francis Ledwidge

When the Dark Cow leaves the moor

Compiled by Liam O'Meara

Francis Ledwidge

The Best Of Francis Ledwidge

'When the Dark Cow leaves the moor'

Edited, with notes by Liam O' Meara

Introduced by Ulick O'Connor

THE INCHICORE LEDWIDGE SOCIETY
RIPOSTE BOOKS

First Published in 2004

RIPOSTE BOOKS
**28 Emmet Road,
Dublin 8.
Ireland**

ISBN: 1901596109

Cover photo shows Ulick O'Connor with Liam O'Meara,
at the National War Memorial Gardens, Islandbridge, Dublin.

Contents

Preface   9
Introduction by Ulick O'Connor   15
Behind The Closed Eye   19
A Moving Picture   21
To A Linnet In A Cage   22
Ode To The Miller   23
To Chanticleer   24
Before The War Of Cooley   25
Imitation Of A Connaught Love Song   27
Thoughts At The Trysting Stile   28
Before The Tears   30
To Lord Dunsany   31
To Matty McGoona   32
The Burial Of Love   33
The Wife Of Llew   34
A Song   35
A Fear   36
Growing Old   37
A Twilight In Middle March   38
God's Remembrance   39
Sleep O Grief Of Me   40
The Lost Ones   41
The Sister   42
June   43
The Singer's Muse   44
August   45
A Little Boy In The Morning   46
The Watcher Of The Sea   47
A Prayer   48
To Lizzie   49
The Call To Ireland   50
To My Little Nephew Seumas   51
Evening In England   52
May   53
The Place   54

To One Dead	55
When Love And Beauty Wander Away	56
The Cobbler Of Sari Gueul	57
The Departure Of Proserpine	59
The Homecoming Of The Sheep	61
My Mother	62
The Shadow People	63
Thomas McDonagh	64
Evening Clouds	65
Manchester	66
Jeu d'Esprit	67
The Herons	68
The Wedding Morning	69
The Blackbirds	70
After Court Martial	71
Ireland	72
To A Sparrow	73
War	74
Last May	75
Old Letters	76
Derry	77
At Currabwee	78
The Dead Kings	79
Had I A Golden Pound	81
A Soldier's Grave	82
In A Café	83
Soliloquy	84
Ascension Thursday, 1917	85
O'Connell Street	86
The Old Gods	87
To A German Officer	88
Home	89
Notes	91

Acknowledgments

A special thanks to our patron, Mr. Joseph Ledwidge; to Lord and Lady Dunsany; to Mr Ulick O'Connor for his support, advice, and his introduction to this new selection; to the members of The Inchicore Ledwidge Society, especially Michael O'Flanagan, our Secretary, and to all those who support us on our annual day of commemoration.

Source List of Quotations and Other References

Back Cover:
Brendan Kennelly, speaking of *Before the War of Cooley*- RTE Radio One, broadcast on 'John Bowman On Saturday,' July, 1997.
Seamus Heaney, from *Poet of the Walking Wounded*- The Irish Times. 21st. Nov. 1992. Con Houlihan, The Irish Press, 1974.
Kevin Myers, from *An Irishman's Diary*, The Irish Times, 27/8/87 and 28/11/1992

Frontispiece, Lance Corp. Francis Ledwidge, April 1915; from original photo., the late Nancy Farrelly.

The manuscript of the poem *'Thomas McDonagh'* is the property of the Trustees of the National Library of Ireland and is specially reproduced here with their permission.

Bibliography

A Lantern On The Wave, A Study Of F.Ledwidge, Riposte Bks., 2000
Francis Ledwidge, The Poems Complete, Goldsmith Press, 1997
Francis Ledwidge, Selected Poems, New Island Books, 1992
Complete Poems of Francis Ledwidge, Martin Brian & O'Keefe 1974
Francis Ledwidge, A Life Of The Poet, Martin Brian & O'Keefe, 1972
Day by Day- Senior, the Educational Company of Ireland.
A Golden Treasury of Irish Verse, Macmillan, London 1925
Patches Of Sunlight, by Lord Dunsany- Heinemann, 1939
The Mabinogion, translated by Lady Charlotte Guest. London, 1904

Thomas McDonagh.

— ✕ —

He shall not hear the bittern cry
In the wild sky, where he is lain,
Nor voices of the sweeter birds
Above the wailing of the rain.

Nor shall he know when loud March blows
Thro' slanting snows his fanfare shrill,
Blowing to flame the golden cup
Of many an upset daffodil.

But when the Dark Cow leaves the moor,
And pastures poor with greedy weeds,
Perhaps he'll hear her low at morn
Lifting her horn in pleasant meads.

F.L.

Preface

On the 30th December 1999, to mark the advent of the new
millennium, the Irish Times listed the one hundred best loved Irish
poems of the century. Theo Dorgan, the then director of Poetry
Ireland, who compiled the chart, remarked on the absence of
Gaelic poems from the list and also, on the poor showing by
today's poets. High on the list of favourite poems was Francis
Ledwidge with two entries, *June* and *Thomas McDonagh,* proving
that he was still as popular as ever.

Remarkably, *Selected Poems* (New Island Books, 1992) was the
first ever selection of the poems of Francis Ledwidge. That fine
book was notable for an introduction by Seamus Heaney and for
Heaney's own tribute to Ledwidge *'In Memoriam Francis
Ledwidge'.* However, as it appeared before the publication of **The
Poems Complete** (Goldsmith Press, 1997) it did not include any of
the 66 poems which I added to the collection at that time. As this
amounts to almost one third of the poet's work, equal in volume to
any two of his original books, it is clear that a selection based on
all of the known poems is now overdue.

This selection acknowledges the wisdom of W.B.Yeats, AE and
Lennox Robinson in their choice of 5 sample poems included in **A
Golden Treasury of Irish Verse*** (Macmillan, London, 1925). The
five poems, *A Twilight in Middle March, The Herons, Thomas
McDonagh, The Blackbirds,* and *August* are all included here. I
have also, respected the views of our eminent Ledwidge enthusi-
asts past and present, from Padraic Colum to Benedict Kiely to
Seamus Heaney, Brendan Kennelly and Dermot Bolger. Noted too,
are the opinions of those who have requested certain poems in the
course of various talks I have given countrywide; in particular,

---

* These were again included in **The Oxford Book of Irish Verse,** edited by Donagh
McDonagh (1958). Other noteworthy inclusions were in **Georgian Poetry** (1913-
1915), Padraic Colum's **Anthology of Irish Verse** (1948), and Robert Farren's **The
Course of Irish Verse** (1948).

these readers will fondly remember *The Shadow People* from the old 'Day By Day' school-book. Finally, there are some of the recently discovered poems including, *The Watcher Of The Sea*, written at Richmond Barracks, a poem that can hold its own with any of the poet's work ; *A Prayer*, of which Ledwidge wrote to Dunsany, *"Fancy that little thing I wrote here with my pen causing a sensation in the Gogarty school."* * ; his controversial poems, *To A German Officer*, written on seeing a wooden cross his comrades had erected over an enemy grave, *Sleep O Grief Of Me* (to an illegitimate child), and *The Old Gods* (To AE), all of which were originally withheld from publication.

As you enjoy reading *The Cobbler of Sari Gueul*, spare a thought: this poem, now considered to be one of his finest, did not appear in the original collection.

The categorisation of Ledwidge's poems has always presented difficulty. Part of the problem is that a large amount of his work was written in Derry in the winter of 1916. There he rewrote from memory many poems lost during his service in Greece and Serbia. Thus, in the original books some poems appear under the heading 'In Barracks,' but have titles such as *Serbia*. Similarly, the poem *O'Connell Street*, describing his return to Dublin in 1916, was actually written in France the following year. To complicate matters further, Alice Curtayne introduced vague and, in some cases, inappropriate headings in her edited update of **Complete Poems** (Martin, Brian and O' Keefe, 1974) which saw the 'McDonagh' poem, for instance, filed under 'Meditative.' Trying to separate the various themes into groups can therefore prove a frustrating and often futile task. Usually, you will find that his themes are interwoven. In the poem *Last May*, he blends a season with the image of his true-love, but he is really speaking about Ireland. Consider this also:

---

*   Dr. Gogarty, however, did point out a minor error, the incorrect use of the word 'lain.' Significantly, Ledwidge thereafter avoided the use of this word until two years later when he used it correctly and to great effect in his most famous poem: *Thomas McDonagh*.

"The lidless eye of noon shall spray
Tan on her ankles in the hay
Shall kiss her brown the whole day long."

This is a description, not of a girl, but of the month of August. Such transference of sexuality onto landscape is typical of Ledwidge. The best example of all, of course, is *Thomas McDonagh,* which uses a pastoral setting for his compassion for a fellow poet and his own sense of patriotism. The whole time he was at the warfront his mind was on the fields and the folk of his native Meath. If that is the way the ideas came to him when he was writing, why should we now attempt to separate his thoughts and feelings? Let us, instead, dip into **The Best of Francis Ledwidge** and experience the beauty and lyricism of a poet who called his poems songs and who gained in his own lifetime the sobriquet 'Poet of the Blackbird.'

Francis Edward Ledwidge, born on the 19th August 1887, the second youngest of nine children was reared in a labourer's cottage in Janeville, Slane, Co. Meath. He left school before the age of 14 to help support his widowed mother by working in the neighbouring farms; later, as a road worker, and for a time in the copper mine at Beauparc. In 1906, he helped found the Slane Branch of the Meath Labour Union, and later became secretary. He also, organized the local Volunteer movement. He had many friends in the Gaelic League having once tried to start a branch in his area. Among these were, Seamus O'Kelly, Seaghan Mac NaMidhe, Seamus O' Sullivan and Thomas McDonagh.

His writing talent eventually came to the attention of Lord Dunsany, landowner and writer of great renown. Dunsany introduced him to the National Literary Society in Dublin and also sent some of his poems to the London publishers. His first collection was being prepared for publication when the First World War began.

Like the majority of people in those days, Ledwidge believed in the ideal of Home Rule. However, he was disheartened when the Home Rule Bill was shelved until after the war. He was one of only six dissidents at a meeting of the Slane corps of volunteers called to vote on the Redmond proposal. At the next Navan Rural Council, all save Ledwidge were in favour of the motion. Frank, who was an elected member of the board, was jeered from all sections of the hall. He left to shouts of *"Traitor"* and *"Coward."* A week later the Board felt obliged to issue an apology and a retraction for the names applied to their fellow member, while noting with some pride that he had since joined the Royal Inniskilling Fusiliers.

Ledwidge announced that he had enlisted: *"... for the fields along the Boyne, for the birds and the blue skies over them."*

He later elaborated:

"I joined the British Army because she stood between Ireland and an enemy common to our civilisation and I would not have her say that she defended us while we did nothing at home but pass resolutions."

The Royal Inniskilling Fusiliers were based at Richmond Barracks in, what is today, the Inchicore area of Dublin. At the end of April, 1915, the Tenth Division were shipped to Basingstoke in England and from there to Gallipoli. Ledwidge survived the disastrous Gallipoli landings and went on to experience active service on the borders of Greece and blizzard bound Serbia, from where the Allies had to make a retreat to Salonika. It was in the course of this march that he collapsed, apparently from exhaustion, but was found to be suffering from inflammation of the gall bladder and had an abscess forming on his liver. Having spent some time in various hospitals in Egypt he was sent back to Manchester and then home, in 1916. As soon as he was deemed fit again for service, he returned to the front and was killed in Flanders on 31st. July, 1917.

When news of his death reached Meath, the Navan Board of Guardians made a stirring tribute to him. One member was even moved to poetry:

'O Poet, child of nature, whose songs we oft have sung, why did you not stay here with us, your own green fields among?'

Why indeed! This reflects not just the hypocrisy shown towards Ledwidge, it reveals the reverse logic and misrepresentation of the 250,000 Irishmen who fought in the Great War; a distortion that began only in the aftermath of the 1916, Easter Rising, was compounded by the intended introduction of conscription in 1918, and gathered momentum thereafter. If a broader, more enlightened, view has been attained today it is in no small measure due to the efforts of such groups as The Royal Dublin Fusiliers Association, The Western Front, and the Irish Soldiers of the First World War Committee (Waterford).

In 2003, The Imperial War Museum included Ledwidge among an exhibition of the works and memorabilia of twelve soldier poets, titled '**Anthem For Doomed Youth**[*].' This was the largest display of its kind ever mounted and ran for six months. It was the first time Ledwidge had been accorded the status of 'War Poet' and joined that canon of poets such as Edmund Blunden, Wilfred Owen, Siegfried Sassoon, Rupert Brook, Edward Thomas, Robert Graves, Isaac Rosenberg, etc. Of course, it should be pointed out that while these poets wrote about war and were involved in a war, as their writings reflect, they were all anti war.

Ledwidge's slim volume, **Songs Of The Fields** had reached him while he was camped on the Serbian slopes. As with his introduction at the National Literary Society in 1914[#], when no fewer than 27 newspapers reported on the event, his first book was welcomed

---

[*]   Taking its name from a manuscript by Wilfred Owen, which Sassoon amended during their stay at Craiglockhart hospital, and which was made famous by Pat Barker's book and the film 'Regeneration.'

[#]   Situated at 6, St. Stephen's Green; today the 'Habitat' store.

with equal enthusiasm. It was acclaimed with laudatory reviews in *The Times, The Standard, Globe, Daily Telegraph, Pall Mall Gazette, Sphere, Manchester Guardian* and all of the top London and Dublin literary journals. The result was that it rapidly sold out and a second impression was printed. Two more collections gathered by his good friend and patron, Lord Dunsany were published posthumously.

He was truly a most remarkable man who lived a mere 29 years, but who nevertheless left behind hundreds of poems, some of which remain, as he, himself, has said *"scattered about two hemispheres."* I have spent the last decade collecting his work. In 1997, to commemorate his eightieth anniversary, I published all of the poems known to me at that time. I will continue in my search for lost poems. In the meantime, enjoy the best of his known works to date.

Liam O'Meara, Chairman,
The Inchicore Ledwidge Society

Introduction

When a poet starts to play around with poppies, linnets and black-birds in his verse it can be dangerous stuff. Keats, Clare, Matthew Arnold and A.E. Housman have been there before and the risk of falling into cliché and losing the plot is considerable...

But a true poet can endow the most ordinary word with the glow of verse. The word 'bent' for instance may seem a little down beat for verse. Yet when Gerald Manly Hopkins uses it in *'God's Grandeur,'* he circum-navigates the universe -

"For the Holy Ghost over the *bent*
World broods with warm breast and with ah! bright wings".

Shakespeare uses an unpromising word like 'stuff' in **The Tempest** to convey an ontological view of the human condition-

"We are such stuff
As dreams are made on; and our little life
Is rounded with a sleep."

Francis Ledwidge can bring this special glow to words. This is from his *'June'*:

"The hedges are all drowned in green grass seas.
And bobbing poppies flare like Elmo's light,
While siren-like the pollen-stained bees
Drone in the clover depths".

Since Herrick, the rose has always been a dangerous flower for all but the most skilful of verse writers to apotheosise. But the last verse of Ledwidge's *'June'* can bring a wistful stab to the heart.

"And loop this red rose in that hazel ring
That snares your little ear. for June is short
And we must joy in it and dance and sing,
And from her bounty draw her rosy worth.
Ay! Soon the swallows will be flying south,
The wind wheel north to gather in the snow,
Even the roses spilt on youth's red mouth
Will soon blow down the road all roses go."

This, from *'A Twilight in Middle March'*:

"And then three syllables of melody
Dropped from a blackbird's flute, and died apart
Far in the dewy dark."

Ledwidge is sometimes thought of as a forgotten poet. This is not so. Poems like these are part of the public's perception of poetry just as Charles Wolfe, Ernest Dowson, and William Cory have lived on without a large body of verse behind them. But it was his death in Belgium in 1917 that undoubtedly deprived the world of a body of poetry which in the opinion of Lord Dunsany would have made Ledwidge the superior of Robert Burns. I remember Lennox Robinson, distinguished Abbey playwright and first director of that theatre, expressing his delight in finding that 1 knew some of Ledwidge's poems off by heart. When Lennox compiled his Palgrave **Golden Treasury of Irish Verse** he had included five of Ledwidge's poems in it.

'Thomas McDonagh' is an extraordinary poem. McDonagh, a professor in the National University and the author of an important book on Anglo-Saxon rhythms had encouraged Ledwidge in the pre first World War years and had been delighted when, probably through the influence of his patron Lord Dunsany, Ledwidge's poems were used by Edward Marsh in his collection of Georgian poetry published in 1915, which included Rupert Brooke and Julian Grenfel. By that time Ledwidge was a soldier in the British army while McDonagh had become a leading figure in the Irish Volunteers and would be executed a year later as one of the leaders

in the Easter Rising. Ledwidge paid him the ultimate tribute in an elegiac poem, of using the difficult internal rhyming scheme of the Gaelic poets as McDonagh had done in his miraculous translation from the Irish of *'The Yellow Bittern.'* The internal rhyme in *'Thomas McDonagh'* creates a resonance like the playing of the flute in an extended musical phrase:

"Nor shall he know when loud March *blows*
Thro' slanting *snows* her fanfare shrill,
Blowing to flame the golden *cup*
Of many an *upset* daffodil."

Nothing I think catches the dilemma of the Irish national mind set as this example of a soldier in British army uniform writing a poem to a friend who had been executed by members of the same army in which he himself was serving. Thomas Kettle MP, killed at Ginchy in the summer of 1916, summed up the sentiment of many Irishmen at that time in his poem to his daughter:

"Know that we fools, now with the foolish dead,
Die not for flag, nor King, nor Emperor,
But for a dream, born in a herdsman's shed.
And for the secret Scripture of the poor."

After the war was over Lord Dunsany loyally saw that Ledwidge's poetry was published in London by Herbert Jenkins. He thus became well known here and in England and was much anthologised, though Yeats did not include him in his **Oxford Book of Modern Verse** which was simply a blunder. How could he have missed this from *'God's Remembrance:'*

And I who am a thought of God's now long
Forgotten in His Mind, and desolate
With other dreams long over, as a gate
Singing upon the wind the anvil song,
Sang of the Spring when first He dreamt of me
In that old town all hills and signs that creak:-

And He remembered me as something far
In old imaginations, something weak
With distance, like a little sparkling star
Drowned in the lavender of evening sea.

There are flaws in some of Ledwidge's poems which one must believe he would have attended to. For instance, this verse occurs in an otherwise good poem *'The Dead Kings:'*

"And one said: "We who yet are kings
Have heard these things lamenting inly."
Sweet music flowed from many a bill
And on the hill the morn stood queenly."

I cannot believe if Ledwidge had lived he would have retained these lines without re-writing them or leaving them out altogether. We should keep this in mind when coming across similar infelicities in his work.

Liam O'Meara, the editor of this selection has stood on guard at the flame of Ledwidge's memory. He and Michael O'Flanagan (editor of the admirable broadsheet **Riposte**) both published poets, have founded the Ledwidge Society of Inchicore which has helped to keep the poet's memory alive. They are most active, and every year have a splendid commemorative ceremony in Luytens beautiful Garden of Remembrance in Kilmainham which is now maintained by the Office of Public Works. This is a true bowery of beauty where nationalists can now genuinely meet and commemorate those of our countrymen who have given their lives in many battlefields home and abroad, that Ireland might one day be ruled by her own.

Ulick O'Connor.

2003, Aug.

Behind The Closed Eye

I walk the old frequented ways
That wind around the tangled braes,
I live again the sunny days
Ere I the city knew.

And scenes of old again are born,
The woodbine lassoing the thorn,
And drooping Ruth-like in the corn
The poppies weep the dew.

Above me in their hundred schools
The magpies bend their young to rules,
And like an apron full of jewels
The dewy cobweb swings.

And frisking in the stream below
The troutlets make the circles flow,
And the hungry crane doth watch them grow
As a smoker does his rings.

Above me smokes the little town,
With its whitewashed walls and roofs of brown
And its octagon[1] spire toned smoothly down
As the holy minds within.

And wondrous, impudently sweet,
Half of him passion, half conceit,

---

[1] Slane Village, known as The Octagon.

The blackbird calls adown the street
Like the piper of Hamelin.

I hear him, and I feel the lure
Drawing me back to the homely moor,
I'll go, and close the mountains' door
On the city's strife and din.

(Circa 1908. Included in a red copybook sent to Lord Dunsany.
Later, Saturday Review, 1912 and Songs of the Fields)

A Moving Picture

She was bending o'er the stream,
Gathering water cresses,
The morning sun did brightly gleam
Through her raven tresses.
The daisies weighed with the dew
Kissed the bank whereon they grew.
O! 'twas a picture grand to view
    In the morning early.

So light she tripped across the brook,
Gathering water cresses,
The sparkling mossy stones scarce shook
So wondrous light her step was.
"Ellie!", 'cross the hill it rang,
The valleys back the echo sang.
—— Deep in my heart I felt love's pang
    In the morning early.

Last night I wandered by that stream,
Gathering water cresses,
With her, the maiden of my theme,
Close in my caresses.
Her dark eyes lifted up to mine
Bespoke of beauty next divine:
—— I woke, the sun did brightly shine
    In the morning early.

(Irish Weekly Independent, 18th. Dec.1909. Later included in the copybook sent to Lord Dunsany in 1912, under the title 'In the Morning Early')

To A Linnet In A Cage

When spring is in the fields that stained your wing,
And the blue distance is alive with song,
And finny quiets of the gabbling spring
Rock lilies red and long,
At dewy daybreak, I will set you free
In ferny turnings of the woodbine lane,
Where faint-voiced echoes leave and cross in glee
The hilly swollen plain.

In draughty houses you forget your tune,
The modulator of the changing hours,
You want the wide air of the moody noon,
And the slanting evening showers.
So I will loose you, and your song shall fall
When morn is white upon the dewy pane,
Across my eyelids, and my soul recall
From worlds of sleeping pain.

(Early poem, later published in Saturday Review,
  March 1913. Songs of the Fields)

Ode To The Miller

Another year heaps fuel on the sun,
And steps upon the busy wheel of time,
Sets his face boldly 'gainst the flying grime
That rises from the grinding grist -
The dust of Man! Oh, list
To how the merry miller sings,
Nor stoppeth morn or eve to take a breath,
But grinds the Youth to Age
The Aged to Death!

(The Drogheda Independent, December 30th. 1911.
  The Poems Complete, 1997)

To Chanticleer

Thou gaudy bird that stalks in pride
About the farmyard all day long,
A legend tells at Christmastide
You heard the angels' song;
And that you flew to Mary's side
When first the mystic starlight shone,
And sent the message far and wide
Chanticleer - "Mac na Máire slán".

And when to Egypt's balmy plain,
Joseph and Mary took their King,
Tho' raved the sleety hurricane
And Winter flung its sling -
They say you followed in their wake,
'Tis Christ from danger was withdrawn,
Thy golden news again did break,
Chanticleer - "Mac na Máire slán".

And still when in the lonely tomb
The mangled form of Jesus lay,
And all the world was wrapped in gloom,
You watched by night and day.
And when the Easter morning broke,
And danced the sun upon the dawn,
O'er the risen Christ again you spoke,
Chanticleer - "Mac Na Máire slán".

(The Drogheda Independent, December 30th. 1911
The Complete Poems, 1974)

Before The War Of Cooley[2]

At daybreak Maeve[3] rose up from where she prayed
And took her prophetess across her door
To gaze upon her hosts. Tall spear and blade
Burnished for early battle dimly shook
The morning's colours, and then Maeve said:
                                                "Look
And tell me how you see them now."
                                        And then
The woman that was lean with knowledge said:
"There's crimson on them, and there's dripping red."
And a tall soldier galloped up the glen
With foam upon his boot, and halted there
Beside old Maeve. She said, "Not yet," and turned
Into her blazing dun, and knelt in prayer
One solemn hour, and once again she came
And sought her prophetess. With voice that mourned,
"How do you see them now? she asked.
                                        "All lame
And broken in the noon." And once again
The soldier stood before her.
                                "No, not yet."
Maeve answered his inquiring look and turned
Once more unto her prayer, and yet once more
"How do you see them now?" she asked.
                                        "All wet
With storm rains, and all broken, and all tore
With midnight wolves." And when the soldier came

---

[2] Cuailnge, county Louth.

[3] Queen Meadhbh of Cruachain (Roscommon).

Maeve said, "It is the hour." There was a flash
Of trumpets in the dim, a silver flame
Of rising shields, loud words passed down the ranks,
And twenty feet they saw the lances leap.
They passed the dun with one short noisy dash.
And turning, proud Maeve gave the wise one thanks,
And sought her chamber in the dún to weep.

(Songs of the Fields)

Imitation Of A Connaught[4] Love Song

He passed my window before the day.
(I'd know his step if the world went by.)
He passed in the dark and went away,
And what is there left to a girl but die?

I thought he was going to Usnagh fair,
And I called and said we would meet at ten.
I might know from the sob in his talking there,
His way was the waters with sailing men.

He wrote me a letter and there he told
He would bring me an apron o' wealth in a year,
As if I cared for the yellow gold,
If only himself and his love were here.

And he won't come over the ocean home,
Tho' I write and write he will not reply.
I'm tired of the world and people who roam.
I will lay me down on my bed and die.

(Circa 1913-14. The Complete Poems 1974)

---

[4] Also, Connacht. It is likely that Ledwidge was influenced by Douglas Hyde's,
'Love Songs Of Connacht.'

Thoughts At The Trysting Stile

Come, May, and hang a white flag on each thorn,
Make truce with earth and heaven; the April child
Now hides her sulky face deep in the morn
Of your new flowers by the water wild
And in the ripples of the rising grass,
And rushes bent to let the south wind pass
On with her tumult of swift nomad wings,
And broken domes of downy dandelion.
Only in spasms now the blackbird sings.
The hour is all a-dream.
                  Nets of woodbine
Throw woven shadows over dreaming flowers,
And dreaming, a bee-luring lily bends
Its tender bell where blue dyke-water cowers
Thro' briars, and folded ferns, and gripping ends
Of wild convolvulus.
               The larks' sky-way
Is desolate.
            I watch an apple-spray
Beckon across a wall as if it knew
I wait the calling of the orchard maid.

Inly I feel that she will come in blue,
With yellow on her hair, and two curls strayed
Out of her comb's loose stocks, and I shall steal
Behind and lay my hands upon her eyes,
"Look not, but be my Psyche!"
                And her peal

Of laughter will ring far, and as she tries
For freedom I will call her names of flowers
That climb up walls; then thro' the twilight hours
We'll talk about the loves of ancient queens,
And kisses like wasp-honey, false and sweet,
And how we are entangled in love's snares
Like wind-looped flowers.

(Songs of the Fields)

Before The Tears

You looked as sad as an eclipsed moon
Above the sheaves of harvest, and there lay
A tight lisp on your tongue, and very soon
The petals of your deep blush fell away;
White smiles that come with an uneasy grace
From inner sorrow crossed your forehead fair
When the wind passing took your scattered hair
And flung it like a brown shower in my face.

Tear-fringed winds that fill the heart's low sighs
And never break upon the bosom's pain,
But blow unto the windows of the eyes
Their misty promises of silver rain,
Around your loud heart ever rose and fell.
I thought 'twere better that the tears should come
And strike your every feeling wholly numb,
So thrust my hand in yours and shook farewell.

(Songs of the Fields)

To Lord Dunsany
(On His Return from East Africa)

For you I knit these lines, and on their ends
Hang little tossing bells to ring you home.
The music is all cracked, the Poesy tends
To richer blooms than mine; but you who roam
Thro' coloured gardens of the highest muse,
And leave the door ajar sometimes that we
May steal small breathing things of reds and blues
And things of white sucked empty by the bee,
Will listen to this bunch of bells from me.

My cowslips ring you welcome to the land
Your muse brings honour to in many a tongue,
Not only that I long to clasp your hand,
But that you're missed by poets who have sung
And viewed with doubt the music of their verse
All the long winter, for you love to bring
The true note in and say the wise thing terse,
And show what birds go lame upon a wing,
And where the weeds among the flowers do spring.

(Dec. 29th. 1913. The Drogheda Independent.
Songs of the Fields)

To Matty McGoona

(Who came one day when we were all gloomy
and cheered us with sad music)

We were all sad and could not weep,
Because our sorrow had not tears:
You came a silent thing like Sleep,
    And stole away our fears

Old memories knocking at each heart
Troubled us with the world's great lie:
You sat a little way apart
    And made a fiddle cry.

And April with her sunny showers
Came laughing up the fields again:
White wings went flashing thro' the hours
    So lately full of pain.

And rivers full of little lights
Came down the fields of waving green:
Our immemorial delights
    Stole in on us unseen.

For this, may Good Luck let you loose
Upon her treasures many years,
And Peace unfurl her flag of truce
    To any threat'ning fears.

(The Drogheda Independent, January 4th. 1914.
Later Included in Songs of the Fields)

The Burial Of Love

We stood and watched the full blown moon arise,
And then I felt her pulse strong in her palm:
I knew the storm was over, and the calm
Would empty out the sorrow in her eyes.
And I then said 'Since this is Love's demise
Our hearts have tears her beauty to embalm,
We'll leave her by forever with a psalm
Of lost promise, in our memories.
And there she shall be clothed in the white
Of our best moments, and the heart shall wear
A path around her grave.' A little sail
Stood on the middle of the moon's huge light,
And for a little while went trembling there,
Believing how the world was waxing pale.

(January 10th. 1914. The Complete Poems, 1974)

The Wife Of Llew

And Gwydion[5] said to Math[6], when it was Spring:
"Come now and let us make a wife for Llew[7]."
And so they broke broad boughs yet moist with dew,
And in a shadow made a magic ring:
They took the violet and the meadowsweet
To form her pretty face, and for her feet
They built a mound of daisies on a wing,
And for her voice they made a linnet sing
In the wide poppy blowing for her mouth.
And over all they chanted twenty hours.
And Llew came singing from the azure south
And bore away his wife of birds and flowers.

(Songs of the Fields)

---

[5] Magician, similar to Merlin, who features in the Mabinogion-Welsh myths of the 12/14th century AD

[6] Math Fab Mathonwyy: god of wealth who could only exist in the human world if his feet were resting on the lap of a virgin.

[7] Llew Llaw Gyffes, son of Gwydion.

A Song

My heart has flown on wings to you, away
In the lonely places where your footsteps lie
Full up of stars when the short showers of day
Have passed like ancient sorrows. I would fly
To your green solitude of woods to hear
You singing in the sounds of leaves and birds;
But I am sad below the depth of words
That nevermore we two shall drew anear.

Had I but wealth of land and bleating flocks
And barnfuls of the yellow yield,
And a large house with climbing hollyhocks
And servant maidens singing in the field,
You'd love me; but I own no roaming herds,
My only wealth is songs of love for you,
And now that you are lost I may pursue
A sad life deep below the depth of words.

(June 1914. Songs of the Fields)

A Fear

I roamed the woods today and seemed to hear,
As Dante heard the voice of suffering trees.
The twisted roots seemed bare contorted knees,
The bark was full of faces strange with fear.

I hurried home still wrapt in that dark spell,
And all the night upon the world's great lie
I pondered, and a voice seemed whisp'ring nigh
"You died long since, and all this thing is hell!"

(Songs of the Fields)

Growing Old

We'll fill a Provence bowl and pledge us deep
The memory of the far ones, and between
The soothing pipes, in heavy-lidded sleep,
Perhaps we'll dream the things that once have been.
'Tis only noon and still too soon to die,
Yet we are growing old, my heart and I.

A hundred books are ready in my head
To open out where Beauty bent a leaf.
What do we want with Beauty? We are wed
Like ancient Proserpine to dismal grief.
And we are changing with the hours that fly,
And growing odd and old, my heart and I.

Across a bed of bells the river flows,
And roses dawn, but not for us; we want
The new thing ever as the old thing grows
Spectral and weary on the hills we haunt.
And that is why we feast, and that is why
We're growing odd and old, my heart and I.

(March 13th. 1914. Songs of the Fields)

A Twilight In Middle March

Within the oak a throb of pigeon wings
Fell silent, and a grey twilight hushed the fold,
And spiders' hammocks swung on half-oped things
That shook like foreigners upon our cold.
A gypsy lit a fire and made a sound
Of moving tins, and from an oblong moon
The river seemed to gush across the ground
To the cracked metre of a marching tune.

And then three syllables of melody
Dropped from the blackbird's flute, and died apart
Far in the dewy dark. No more but three,
Yet sweeter music never touched a heart
'Neath the blue domes of London. Flute and reed,
Suggesting feelings of the solitude
When will was all the Delphi I would heed,
Lost like a wind within a summer wood
From little knowledge where great sorrows brood.

(March 16 th. 1914. Songs of the Fields)

God's Remembrance

There came a whisper from the night to me
Like music of the sea, a mighty breath
From out the valley's dewy mouth, and Death
Shook his lean bones, and every coloured tree
Wept in the fog of morning. From the town
Of nests among the branches one old crow
With gaps upon his wings flew far away.
And, thinking of the golden summer glow,
I heard a blackbird whistle half his lay
Among the spinning leaves that slanted down.

And I who am a thought of God's now long
Forgotten in His Mind, and desolate
With other dreams long over, as a gate
Singing upon the wind the anvil song,
Sang of the Spring when first He dreamt of me
In that old town all hills and signs that creak-
And He remembered me as something far
In old imaginations, something weak
With distance, like a little sparkling star
Drowned in the lavender of evening sea.

(March 22nd. 1914. Songs of the Fields)

Sleep O Grief Of Me

Sleep, O grief of me, and living sin
Of your false father, tho' the blame is sore
Upon my conscience, motherhood will win
Delights for you, and make a golden store
Of laughter for your cheeks. I'll bring you ways
Of sunset paths on water, and will scoop
The stars from out the puddles, and the day's
Wet rainbow for a hoop.

Sleep beauty scorned, sleep little twilight eyes,
The unborn Christ made Joseph doubt his wife.
God never meant you for a mother's sighs,
Only He wants you would He give you life?
Hear not their cants, but list your mother sing,
My love shall shield you like an angel's wing.

(May 1914. The Poems Complete 1997)

The Lost Ones

Somewhere is music from the linnet's bills,
And thro' the sunny flowers the bee-wings drone,
And white bells of convolvulus on hills
Of quiet May make silent ringing, blown
Hither and thither by the wind of showers,
And somewhere all the wandering birds have flown:
And the brown breath of Autumn chills the flowers.

But where are all the loves of long ago?
Oh, little twilight ship blown up the tide,
Where are the faces laughing in the glow
Of morning years, the lost ones scattered wide?
Give me your hand, oh brother, let us go
Crying about the dark for those who died.

(Songs of the Fields)

The Sister

I saw the little quiet town,
And the whitewashed gables on the hill,
And laughing children coming down
The laneway to the mill.

Wind-blushes up their faces glowed,
And they were happy as could be,
The wobbling water never flowed
So merry and so free.

One little maid withdrew aside
To pick a pebble from the sands.
Her golden hair was long and wide,
And there were dimples on her hands.

And when I saw her large blue eyes,
What was the pain that went thro' me?
Why did I think on Southern skies
And ships upon the sea?

(Songs of the Fields)

June

Broom out the floor now, lay the fender by,
And plant this bee-sucked bough of woodbine there,
And let the window down. The butterfly
Floats in upon the sunbeam, and the fair
Tanned face of June, the nomad gypsy, laughs
Above her widespread wares, the while she tells
The farmer's fortunes in the fields, and quaffs
The water from the spider-peopled wells.

The hedges are all drowned in green grass seas,
And bobbing poppies flare like Elmo's light,
While siren-like the pollen-stainéd bees
Drone in the clover depths. And up the height
The cuckoo's voice is hoarse and broke with joy.
And on the lowland crops the crows make raid,
Nor fear the clappers of the farmer's boy,
Who sleeps, like drunken Noah, in the shade.

And loop this red rose in that hazel ring
That snares your little ear, for June is short
And we must joy in it and dance and sing,
And from her bounty draw her rosy worth.
Ay! soon the swallows will be flying south,
The wind wheel north to gather in the snow,
Even the roses spilt on youth's red mouth
Will soon blow down the road all roses go.

(Songs of the Fields)

The Singer's Muse

I brought in these to make her kitchen sweet,
Haw blossoms and the roses of the lane.
Her heart seemed in her eyes so wild they beat
With welcome for the boughs of Spring again.
She never heard of Babylon or Troy,
She read no book, but once saw Dublin town;
Yet she made a poet of her servant boy
And from Parnassus earned the laurel crown.

If Fame, the Gorgon, turns me into stone
Upon some city square, let someone place
Thorn blossoms and lane roses newly blown
Beside my feet, and underneath them trace:
"His heart was like a bookful of girls' song,
With little loves and mighty Care's alloy.
These did he bring his muse, and suffered long,
Her bashful singer and her servant boy."

(July 1914. Songs of the Fields)

44

August

She'll come at dusky first of day,
White over yellow harvest's song.
Upon her dewy rainbow way
She shall be beautiful and strong.
The lidless eye of noon shall spray
Tan on her ankles in the hay,
Shall kiss her brown the whole day long.

I'll know her in the windrows, tall
Above the crickets of the hay.
I'll know her when her odd eyes fall,
One May-blue, one November-grey.
I'll watch her from the red barn wall
Take down her rusty scythe, and call,
And I will follow her away.

(August 1914. Songs of the Fields)

A Little Boy In The Morning

He will not come, and still I wait.
He whistles at another gate
Where angels listen. Ah, I know
He will not come, yet if I go
How shall I know he did not pass
Barefooted in the flowery grass?

The moon leans on one silver horn
Above the silhouettes of morn,
And from their nest-sills finches whistle
Or stooping pluck the downy thistle.
How is the moon so gay and fair
Without his whistling in its air?

The world is calling, I must go.
How shall I know he did not pass
Barefooted in the shining grass?

(December 1914. Songs of Peace)

The Watcher Of The Sea

The head of Bran[8] was watching for us lest
The foe should steal on us while we did toil
For manumission to the East and West,
Planting the bread upon the savage soil.
Why are you silent still, five magic birds?
You had sweet music when your laughter ran
In ripples up his face to all his scars,
The hundred years we talked his many wars;
Sing one more song before the face of Bran.

It is not ours to conquer, but defend,
The brightest emprise of our lives is this,
At home to prosper and abroad befriend
The nations rising thro' the drear abyss,
Where slavery makes a noise of chains, and herds
Of sun-dark people moan from child to man.
Sing this before the watcher of the sea,
Five magic birds till all the world is free,
And praise aloud the faithful head of Bran.

(Richmond Barracks, Dec. 1914. The Poems Complete, 1997)

---

[8] Gigantic Celtic deity (son of Llyr) who features in the Mabinogion, a collection of
medieval Welsh tales. See end notes.

A Prayer

Ah, let our hearts alone, Pale Christ, we tire,
Of ever moaning with You, too much pain
You tell us of, too much of one desire.
I love You for Your suffering Love. I've lain
My head upon Your wounds, and why destroy
My heavenly confidence with threats of Hell?
How can You threaten us Who loved so well?
You've buoyed up Peter, still my poor Faith buoy.

You've asked me for my heart, it is not mine.
The world drew lots for it before You came,
How can I bargain with You then and dine
Upon Your bread and gall? Ah, shall Your flame
Of Nether persecute me? Like Lot's wife
Turning to you I lost, I am become
A pillar weeping for a lost desire,
A phoenix building up its funeral pyre.
A blind man praying for a Mercy dumb.

Ah, let my heart alone and I will bring
Ten talents back for this poor one of song.
If ever it lay buried when the sting
Of sorrow pained my soul it blossomed strong
For one small Hope. Ah, let my heart alone,
Nor persecute it with Your Love. Believe
That I have loved Your Death, have loved Your Pain.
But these are past and why should You again
Make our hearts Calvary wherein to grieve?

(Richmond Barracks, 1915. The Poems Complete, 1997)

To Lizzie

I'd make my heart a harp to play for you
Love songs within the two dim dusks of day,
Were it not dumb with ache and with mildew
Of sorrow withered like a flower away.
It hears so many calls from homeland places,
So many sighs from all it must remember,
From the pale roads and woodlands where your face is
Like laughing sunlight running thro' December.

But this it whispers still for all its pain,
To bring the greater ache, what may befall
The love that oft-times woke the sweeter strain
Shall turn to you always. And should you call,
To pity it some day in those old places,
Angels will covet the loud joy that fills it. ——
—— But thinking of the bye-ways where your face is
Sunlight on other hearts, Ah! how it kills it.

(Richmond Barracks, 10th. Feb. 1915. This version: The Poems Complete, 1997. cf. Songs of Peace.)

The Call To Ireland

It's time to be up and be doing,
To be up and be doing now;
For, lo, anywhere around you,
From the vale to the mountains brow,
The grass grows up through the harrow,
And the weather rusts on the plough.
Oh, let us be up and be doing
The work that is calling us now.

We have fought so much for the nation
In the tents we helped to divide;
Shall the cause of our common fathers
On our hearthstones lie denied?
For the price of a field we have wrangled
While the weather rusted the plough,
'Twas yours and 'twas mine, but 'tis ours yet
And it's time to be fencing it now.

There is gall in the cups of our children,
But ours is the goblet of wine.
They are crying away in the future:
Is their cause neither yours nor mine?
Better they die in their mothers
Than our shame be writ on their brow,
If we will not be up and be doing
The work that is calling us now.

(The Irish Times, sent from Richmond Barracks, Feb. 12th. 1915. The Poems Complete, 1997)

To My Little Nephew Seumas[9]
(The Child Of Dreams)

I will bring you all the colours
Of the snail box when I come,
And shells that you may listen
To a distant ocean's hum.
And from the rainbow's bottom
I will bring you coloured lights
To scare away the banshees
That cry in the nights.

And I will sing you strange songs
Of places far away,
Where little moaning waters
Have wandered wild astray;
'Til you shall see the bell flowers
Shaking in the breeze,
Thinking they are ringing them
The short way to the seas.

When I come back from wand'ring
It's a strange man I'll be,
And first you'll be a bit afraid
To climb upon my knee.
But when you see the rare gifts
I've gathered you, it seems
You'll leave your head upon me
And travel in your dreams.

(April 1915. The Complete Poems, 1974)

---

[9] Son of the poet's sister, Mary.

Evening In England

From its blue vase the rose of evening drops.
Upon the streams its petals float away.
The hills all blue with distance hide their tops
In the dim silence falling on the grey.
A little wind said "Hush!" and shook a spray
Heavy with May's white crop of opening bloom,
A silent bat went dipping up the gloom.

Night tells her rosary of stars full soon,
They drop from out her dark hand to her knees.
Upon a silhouette of woods the moon
Leans on one horn as if beseeching ease
From all her changes which have stirred the seas.
Across the ears of Toil Rest throws her veil,
I and a marsh bird only make a wail.

(In camp at Basingstoke, May 1915. Songs of Peace)

May

She leans across an orchard gate somewhere,
Bending from out the shadows to the light,
A dappled spray of blossom in her hair
Studded with dew-drops lovely from the night.
She smiles to think how many hearts she'll smite
With beauty ere her robes fade from the lawn.
She hears the robin's cymbals with delight,
The skylark in the rosebush of the dawn.

For her the cowslip rings its yellow bell,
For her violets watch with wide blue eyes.
The wandering cuckoo doth its clear name tell
Thro' the white mist of blossoms where she lies
Painting a sunset for the western skies.
You'd know her by her smile and by her tear
And by the way the swift and martin flies,
Where she is south of these wild days and drear.

(Basingstoke, May 1915. Songs of Peace)

The Place

Blossoms as old as May I scatter here,
And a blue wave I lifted from the stream.
It shall not know when winter days are drear
Or March is hoarse with blowing. But a-dream
The laurel boughs shall hold a canopy
Peacefully over it the winter long,
Till all the birds are back from oversea,
And April rainbows win a blackbird's song.

And when the war is over I shall take
My lute a-down to it and sing again
Songs of the whispering things amongst the brake,
And those I love shall know them by their strain.
Their airs shall be the blackbird's twilight song,
Their words shall be all flowers with fresh dews hoar -
But it is lovely now in winter long,
And God! to hear the blackbird sing once more.

(Basingstoke, 1915. Songs of Peace)

To One Dead

A blackbird singing
On a moss-upholstered stone,
Bluebells swinging,
Shadows wildly blown,
A song in the wood,
A ship on the sea.
The song was for you
And the ship was for me.

A blackbird singing
I hear in my troubled mind,
Bluebells swinging
I see in a distant wind.
But sorrow and silence
Are the wood's threnody,
The silence for you
And the sorrow for me.

(Basingstoke, 1915. Songs of Peace)

When Love And Beauty Wander Away

When Love and Beauty wander away,
And there's no more hearts to be sought and won,
When the old earth limps thro' the dreary day,
And the work of the Seasons cry undone:
Ah! what shall we do for a song to sing,
Who have known Beauty, and Love, and Spring?

When Love and Beauty wander away,
And a pale fear lies on the cheeks of youth,
When there's no more goal to strive for and pray,
And we live at the end of the world's untruth:
Ah! what shall we do for a heart to prove,
Who have known Beauty, and Spring, and Love?

(November, 1915. Songs of Peace)

The Cobbler Of Sari Gueul

A cobbler lives in Sari Gueul
Who has a wise mind, people say.
He sits in his door on a three-legged stool,
Hammering leather all the day.
He laughs with the boys who make such noise
And loves to watch how the children play.
Gladly I'd shuffle my lot in a pool
With that of the cobbler of Sari Gueul.

Sorrow to him is a ball of wax
That melts in the sun of a cheerful smile
And all his needs are, a box of tacks,
Thread and leather, old boots in a pile.
I would give my art for half of his heart.
Who wants the world with all its guile?
And which of us two is the greater fool,
Me, or the cobbler of Sari Gueul?

At evening an old cow climbs the street,
So lean and bony you'd wonder how.
He hears the old cracked bell from his seat
And the wrinkles move on his yellow brow,
And he says as he strikes, 'To me or my likes
You are coming faster, old brown cow.
Slow steps come fast to the knife and rule.'
Says the wise old cobbler of Sari Gueul.

Often I hear him in my sleep,
Hammering still in the little town.

And I see the queer old shops on the steep,
And the queerer folk move up and down.
And the cobbler's sign creaks up in a vine,
When the wind slips over the housetops brown.
Waking, I pray to the Gods who rule
For the queer old cobbler of Sari Gueul.

(Greece, 1915. The Complete Poems)

The Departure Of Proserpine

Old mother earth for me always grieves,
Her morns wake weeping and her noons are dim,
Silence has left her woods, and all the leaves
Dance in the windy shadows on the rim
Of the dull lake thro' which I soon shall pass
        To my dark bridal bed
Down in the hollow chambers of the dead.
Will not the thunder hide me if I call,
Wrapt in the corner of some distant star
The gods have never known?
        Alas! Alas!
My voice has left with the last wing, my fall
Shall crush the flowery fields with gloom, as far
        As swallows fly.
        Would I might die
And in a solitude of roses lie
As the last buds outblown.
Then nevermore Demeter would be heard
Wail in the blowing rain, but every shower
Would come bound up with rainbows to the birds
Wrapt in a dusty wing, and the dry flower
        Hanging a shrivelled lip.
This weary change from light to darkness fills
My heart with twilight, and my brightest day
Dawns over thunder and in thunder spills
        Its urn to gladness
        With a sadness
Through which the slow dews drip
And the bat goes over on a thorny wing.
Is it a dream that once I used to sing

From Aegean shores across her rocky isles,
Making the bells of Babylon to ring
                Over the wiles
That lifted me from darkness to the Spring?
                And the King
Seeing his wine in blossom on the tree
Danced with the Queen a merry roundelay,
And all the blue circumference of the day
Was loud with flying song —
— But let me pass along:
What brooks it the unfree to thus delay?
No secret turning leads from the god's way.

(Greece, Dec.1915. Songs of Peace)

The Homecoming Of The Sheep

The sheep are coming home in Greece,
Hark the bells on every hill!
Flock by flock, and fleece by fleece,
Wandering wide a little piece
Thro' the evening red and still,
Stopping where the pathways cease,
Cropping with a hurried will.

Thro' the cotton-bushes low
Merry boys with shouldered crooks
Close them in a single row,
Shout among them as they go
With one bell-ring o'er the brooks.
Such delight you never know
Reading it from gilded books.

Before the early stars are bright
Cormorants and sea-gulls call,
And the moon comes large and white
Filling with a lovely light
The ferny curtained waterfall.
Then sleep wraps every bell up tight
And the climbing moon grows small.

(Greece, 1915. Songs of Peace)

My Mother

God made my mother on an April day,
From sorrow and the mist along the sea,
Lost birds' and wanderers' songs and ocean spray,
And the moon loved her wandering jealously.

Beside the ocean's din she combed her hair,
Singing the nocturne of the passing ships,
Before her earthly lover found her there
And kissed away the music from her lips.

She came unto the hills and saw the change
That brings the swallow and the geese in turns.
But there was not a grief she deemed strange,
For there is that in her which always mourns.

Kind heart she has for all on hill or wave
Whose hopes grew wings like ants to fly away.
I bless the God Who such a mother gave
This poor bird-hearted singer of a day.

(In hospital In Cairo. March-April 1916)

The Shadow People

Old lame Bridget doesn't hear
Fairy music in the grass
When the gloaming's on the mere
And the shadow people pass:
Never hears their slow grey feet
Coming from the village street
Just beyond the parson's wall,
Where the clover globes are sweet
And the mushroom's parasol
Opens in the moonlit rain.
Every night I hear them call
From their long and merry train.
Old lame Bridget says to me,
'It is just your fancy, child.'
She cannot believe I see
Laughing faces in the wild,
Hands that twinkle in the sedge
Bowing at the water's edge
Where the finny minnows quiver,
Shaping on a blue wave's ledge
Bubble foam to sail the river.
And the sunny hands to me
Beckon ever, beckon ever.
Oh! I would be wild and free
And with the shadow people be.

(Serbia and Egypt. Songs of Peace)

Thomas McDonagh

He shall not hear the bittern cry
In the wild sky, where he is lain,
Nor voices of the sweeter birds
Above the wailing of the rain.

Nor shall he know when loud March blows
Thro' slanting snows her fanfare shrill,
Blowing to flame the golden cup
Of many an upset daffodil.

But when the Dark Cow leaves the moor,
And pastures poor with greedy weeds,
Perhaps he'll hear her low at morn
Lifting her horn in pleasant meads.

(Manchester. May 1916. Songs of Peace)

Evening Clouds

A little flock of clouds go down to rest
In some blue corner off the moon's highway,
With shepherd winds that shook them in the West
To borrowed shapes of earth, in bright array,
Perhaps to weave a rainbow's gay festoons
Around the lonesome isle which Brook[10] has made
A little England full of lovely noons,
Or dot it with his country's mountain shade.

Ah, little wanderers, when you reach that isle
Tell him, with dripping dew, they have not failed,
What he loved most; for late I roamed awhile
Thro' English fields and down her rivers sailed;
And they remember him with beauty caught
From old desires of Oriental Spring
Heard in his heart with singing overwrought;
And still on Purley Common gooseboys sing.

(Songs of Peace)

---

[10] Fellow poet and soldier, Rupert Brook.

Manchester

We went to where gay women danced and sang,
And clever men were juggling with repartees,
And people pleased to see us rowed us down
To fete us at a dozen garden parties.
And while they laughed and talked of some new wonder
Perhaps they thought my coldness most unkind;
How could they know the lovely clock of Derry
Was striking every quarter in my mind.

(Manchester, May 1916. The Poems Complete, 1997)

Jeu d'Esprit

What rumours filled the Atlantic sky,
And turned the wild geese back again;
When Plunkett[11] lifted Balor's[12] eye,
And broke Andromeda's strong chain?
Or did they hear that Starkie, James[13],
Among the gallipots[14] was seen,
And he who called her sweetest names,
Was talking to another queen?

Now all the wise in quicklime burn,
And all the strong have crossed the sea;
But down the pale roads of Ashbourne,
Are heard the voices of the free.
And Jemmy Quigley[15] is the boy,
Could say how queenly was her walk,
When Sackville Street went down like Troy,
And peelers fell in far Dundalk.

*(First published in 'As I Was Going Down Sackville Street'- written by poet
and surgeon, Oliver St. John Gogarty. The Complete Poems.*

---

[11] 1916 leader and signatory of the Irish Proclamation, Joseph Mary Plunkett.
[12] Formorian Cyclops whose evil eye could destroy an army.
[13] James Sullivan Starkie, essayist, poet and editor of The Dublin Magazine; other-
wise known as Seumas O'Sullivan, a close friend of Ledwidge.
[14] Medicine pots: O Sullivan's father was a pharmacist and Seumas had a brief
apprenticeship in the business.
[15] County Surveyor: see end notes.

The Herons

As I was climbing Ardan Mor
From the shore of Sheelan lake,
I met the herons coming down
Before the waters wake.

And they were talking in their flight
Of dreamy ways the herons go
When all the hills are withered up
Nor any waters flow.

(Ebrington Barracks, Derry 1916. Songs of Peace)

The Wedding Morning

Spread the feast, and let there be
Such music heard as best beseems
A king's son coming from the sea
To wed a maiden of the streams.

Poets, pale for long ago,
Bring sweet sounds from rock and flood,
You, by echo's accent know
Where the water is and wood.

Harpers whom the moths of Time
Bent and wrinkled dusty brown,
Her chains are falling with a chime,
Sweet as bells in Heaven town.

But, harpers, leave your harps aside,
And, poets, leave awhile your dreams.
The storm has come upon the tide
And Cathleen weeps among her streams.

(Ebrington Barracks, Derry 1916. Songs of Peace)

The Blackbirds

I heard the Poor Old Woman say:
'At break of day the fowler came,
And took my blackbirds from their songs
Who loved me well thro' shame and blame.

No more from lovely distances
Their songs shall bless me mile by mile,
Nor to white Ashbourne call me down
To wear my crown another while.

With bended flowers the angels mark
For the skylark the place they lie,
From there its little family
Shall dip their wings first in the sky.

And when the first surprise of flight
Sweet songs excite, from the far dawn
Shall there come blackbirds loud with love,
Sweet echoes of the singers gone.

But in the lonely hush of eve
Weeping I grieve the silent bills'
I heard the Poor Old Woman say
In Derry of the little hills.

(Ebrington Barracks, July 1916. Songs of Peace)

After Court Martial

My mind is not my mind, therefore
I take no heed of what men say,
I lived ten thousand years before
God cursed the town of Nineveh.

The Present is a dream I see
Of horror and loud sufferings,
At dawn a bird will waken me
Unto my place among the kings.

And though men called me a vile name,
And all my dream companions gone,
'Tis I the soldier bears the shame,
Not I the king of Babylon.

(Ebrington Barracks, 1916. Last Songs)

Ireland

I called you by sweet names by wood and linn,
You answered not because my voice was new,
And you were listening for the hounds of Finn
    And the long hosts of Lugh.

And so, I came unto a windy height
And cried my sorrow, but you heard no wind,
For you were listening to small ships in flight,
    And the wail on hills behind.

And then I left you, wandering the war
Armed with will, from distant goal to goal,
To find you at the last free as of yore,
    Or die to save your soul.

And then you called to us from far and near
To bring your crown from out the deeps of time,
It is my grief your voice I couldn't hear
    In such a distant clime.

(Derry 1916, Last Songs)

To A Sparrow

Because you have no fear to mingle
Wings with those of greater part,
So like me, with song I single
Your sweet impudence of heart.

And when prouder feathers go where
Summer holds her leafy show,
You still come to us from nowhere
Like grey leaves across the snow.

In back ways where odd and end go
To your meals you drop down sure,
Knowing every broken window
Of the hospitable poor.

There is no bird half so harmless,
None so sweetly rude as you,
None so common and so charmless,
None of virtues nude as you.

But for all your faults I love you,
For you linger with us still,
Though the wintry winds reprove you
And the snow is on the hill.

(Derry, Sept.20th. 1916. Last Songs)

War

Darkness and I are one, and wind
And nagging thunder, brothers all,
My mother was a storm.
                              I call
And shorten your way with speed to me.
I am Love and Hate and the terrible mind
Of vicious gods —— but more am I,
I am the pride in the lover's eye,
I am the epic of the sea.

(Derry, 28th. Oct. 1916. The Complete Poems, 1974)

Last May

I went to meet my love at dark
In Barna Park when May was there,
But nowhere in the night she strayed,
The lovely maid with the silken hair.

By starry pools of fen and wold
Where gods of old are dreaming still
I wandered to the haunts she knew
'Till the moon was due unto the hill.

And just before the pale day-break
Beyond the lake I heard a cry,
As full of moan and wild despair
As fills the air when great men die.

'My love is dead' I made my moan,
'And I'm alone in Barna Park,'
But rising from the dewy corn,
Above the morn I heard the lark.

And from a bye-way blackbird-loud
My love came proudly, sweetly down.
Her step made dew-bows in the grass
So swift she passed to take her crown.

(Derry, Nov. 1916. The Complete Poems, 1974)

Old Letters

Old letters tied with a ribbon of blue,
And dusty with lavender gathered in years
When youth was sunny and love was true,
And life was but laughter to me and you,
And never a thing for tears.

Here faint-winged Cupids are soaring on high,
And slain hearts lie on the scented page.
Oh, how could our love so easily die,
Or were these little dim words a lie
Told in a foolish age?

And you are still in that little town
Of wind-mills, facing the breezy sea.
Is it nothing to you if my heart breaks down
For the smile that turned to a cold dark frown?
Still are you nothing to me?

Old letters scented with summers past
Tied in a ribbon that held your hair,
Sweet with the love that I dreamed would last
'Til the earth be dust in the sounding blast
And one with the worlds that were.

(Derry, Nov. 1916. The Poems Complete, 1997)

Derry

By day a place of wheels and looms
That struggle in a narrow space,
A shout of children in the slums
And girls with labour-stainéd face.

By night a queen with victory crowned,
For all her years of loud turmoil.
She spreads her beauty all around,
Reflects her glory in the Foyle.

(Derry, Nov. 1916. The Complete Poems, 1974)

At Currabwee

Every night at Currabwee
Little men with leather hats
Mend the boots of Faery
From the tough wings of the bats.
So my mother told to me,
And she is wise you will agree.

Louder than a cricket's wing
All night long their hammer's glee
Times the merry songs they sing
Of Ireland glorious and free.
So I heard Joseph Plunkett say,
You know he heard them but last May.

And when the night is very cold
They warm their hands against the light
Of stars that make the waters gold
Where they are labouring all the night.
So Pearse said, and he knew the truth,
Among the stars he spent his youth.

And I, myself, have often heard
Their singing as the stars went by,
For am I not of those who reared
The banner of old Ireland high,
From Dublin town to Turkey's shores,
And where the Vardar loudly roars?

(Derry, Dec. 1916. Last Songs)

The Dead Kings

All the dead kings came to me
At Rosnaree, where I was dreaming,
A few stars glimmered through the morn,
And down the thorn the dews were streaming.

And every dead king had a story
Of ancient glory, sweetly told.
It was too early for the lark,
But the starry dark had tints of gold.

I listened to the sorrows three
Of that Eire passed into song.
A cock crowed near a hazel croft,
And up aloft dim larks winged strong.

And I, too, told the kings a story
Of later glory, her fourth sorrow:
There was a sound like moving shields
In high green fields and lowland furrow.

And one said: "We who yet are kings
Have heard these things lamenting inly."
Sweet music flowed from many a bill
And on the hill the morn stood queenly.

And one said: "Over is the singing,
And bell bough ringing, whence we come;
With heavy hearts we'll tread the shadows,
In honey meadows birds are dumb."

And one said: "Since the poets perished
And all they cherished in the way,
Their thoughts unsung, like petal showers
Inflame the hours of blue and grey."

And one said: "A loud tramp of men
We'll hear again at Rosnaree."
A bomb burst near me where I lay.
I woke, 'twas day in Picardy.

(France, Jan. 7th. 1917. Last Songs)

Had I A Golden Pound

(After the Irish)

Had I a golden pound to spend,
My love should mend and sew no more
And I would buy her a little quern,
Easy to turn on the kitchen floor.

And for her windows curtains white,
With birds in flight and flowers in bloom,
To face with pride the road to town,
And mellow down her sunlit room.

And with the silver change we'd prove
The truth of Love to life's own end,
With hearts the years could but embolden,
Had I a golden pound to spend.

(France, Feb. 5th. 1917. Last Songs)

A Soldier's Grave

Then in the lull of midnight, gentle arms
Lifted him slowly down the slopes of death,
Lest he should hear again the mad alarms
Of battle, dying moans and painful breath.

And where the earth was soft for flowers we made
A grave for him that he might better rest.
So, Spring shall come and leave it sweet arrayed,
And there the lark shall turn her dewy nest.

(France, 10th. Feb. 1917. The Complete Poems, 1974)

In A Café

Kiss the maid and pass her round,
Lips like hers were made for many.
Our loves are far from us tonight,
But these red lips are sweet as any.

Let no empty glass be seen
Aloof from our good table's sparkle,
At the acme of our cheer
Here are francs to keep the circle.

They are far who miss us most ——
Sip and kiss —— how well we know them,
Battling through the world to keep
Their hearts at peace, their God above them.

(France, Feb. 11th. 1917. Last Songs)

Soliloquy

When I was young I had a care
Lest I should cheat me of my share
Of that which makes it sweet to strive
For life, and dying still survive,
A name in sunshine written higher
Than lark or poet dare aspire.

But I grew weary doing well,
Besides, 'twas sweeter in that hell,
Down with the loud banditti people
Who robbed the orchards, climbed the steeple
For jackdaws' eggs and made the cock
Crow ere 'twas daylight on the clock.
I was so very bad the neighbours
Spoke of me at their daily labours.

And now I'm drinking wine in France,
The helpless child of circumstance.
Tomorrow will be loud with war,
How will I be accounted for?

It is too late now to retrieve
A fallen dream, too late to grieve
A name unmade, but not too late
To thank the gods for what is great;
A keen-edged sword, a soldier's heart,
Is greater than a poet's art.
And greater than a poet's fame
A little grave that has no name,
Whence honour turns away in shame.

(France. Last Songs)

Ascension Thursday, 1917

Lord, Thou hast left Thy footprints in the rocks,
That we may know the way to follow Thee,
But there are wide lands opened out between
Thy Olivet and my Gethsemane.

And oftentimes I make the night afraid,
Crying for lost hands when the dark is deep,
And strive to reach the sheltering of Thy love
Where Thou art herd among Thy folded sheep.

Thou wilt not ever thus, O Lord, allow
My feet to wander when the sun is set,
But through the darkness, let me still behold
The stony bye-ways up to Olivet.

(France, 31ˢᵗ. May 1917. First published in 'The Years of the Shadow'-
Katherine Tynan, 1919. The Complete Poems, 1974)

O' Connell Street

A noble failure is not vain,
But hath a victory its own.
A bright delectance from the slain
Is down the generations thrown.

And, more than Beauty understands,
Has made her lovelier here, it seems.
I see white ships that crowd her strands,
For mine are all the dead men's dreams.

(France, June 10th. 1917. The Complete Poems, 1974)

The Old Gods

I thought the old gods still in Greece
Making the little fates of man,
So in a secret place of peace
I prayed as but a poet can:

And all my prayer went crying faint
Around Parnassus'[16] cloudy height,
And found no ear for my complaint,
And back unanswered came at night.

Ah, foolish that I was to heed
The voice of folly, or presume
To find the old gods in my need,
So far from AE's little room.

*(France, June 10th. 1917. First published in 'The Years of the Shadow' -
Katherine Tynan, 1919. The Poems Complete 1997)*

---

[16] Mount Parnassus, Delphi, where was situated the Temple of the Oracle of Apollo.

To A German Officer

who died a true gentleman

I cannot think that God could take
A man who fought on Mammon's side
Nor yet in brimstone caverns break
A noble soul's ancestral pride.

There is a No-Man's-Land, I hold,
Kept by a truce of Heaven and Hell,
And in their dug-outs made of gold
The brave of these forever dwell.

And greater peace than swords have sought
Flashing in emprises divine
Shuts up their memories in one thought
That hears the quiet waves of the Rhine.

(Belgium, July 1917. The Poems Complete, 1997)

Home

A burst of sudden wings at dawn,
Faint voices in a dreamy noon,
Evenings of mist and murmurings,
And nights with rainbows of the moon.

And through these things a wood-way dim,
And waters dim, and slow sheep seen
On uphill paths that wind away
Through summer sounds and harvest green.

This is a song a robin sang
This morning on a broken tree,
It was about the little fields
That call across the world to me.

(Belgium, July 1917. Last Songs)

Notes

19 Behind the Closed Eye
The poem that caught the attention of Lord Dunsany. Ledwidge once worked as an apprentice in a vintners and grocery shop, W.T. Daly's in Rathfarnham. After only six days he grew homesick and one night stole out quietly and began a thirty mile walk back to Meath. *" I wish to say that this little poem was framed up before I reached the age of sixteen, four years ago, when I was at business in the city of Dublin"* -a quote from a red copybook sent to Lord Dunsany in 1912. Simple mathematics proves that in the summer of 1908 Ledwidge was in fact 20 years old.
In the town of Slane, four large Georgian houses stand at the intersection of the Dublin/Derry and Drogheda/Navan roads. The houses are angled towards one another in a way that creates an octagon. In earlier times the area was known as 'the octagon.' Thus, when Ledwidge referred to the 'octagon' spire he meant the spire within the octagon, or village. In his time the spire was completely clad in ivy with just the smoothed down top and cross showing.

21 A Moving Picture
This poem was addressed to local girl Ellie Vaughey. The poet got to know her through his friendship with her brother Paddy. This is the earliest reference to her and the only time he called her by name in a poem. It may well be, that she saw the poem and was embarrassed by the fact that he had shouted her name not just across the valleys, but across the pages of the newspaper. Thereafter, her identity was hidden under vague descriptions such as 'the orchard maid,' etc. Ellie's two grand-daughters laid a wreath in honour of the poet at the War Memorial Park in Dublin as part of The Inchicore Ledwidge Society's annual commemoration on 27th. July 2003.

23 Ode to the Miller
24 To Chanticleer
Both poems appeared in the same issue of The Drogheda Independent, Dec.30th 1911. This was unusual and showed that the poet's star was on the rise even before he met Dunsany.

25 Before the War of Cooley
Refers to the Tain Bo Cuailnge, or great cattle raids, in the Ulster Cycle; in particular, the Donn Cuailnge, a great bull taken by Meadhbh after its owner, Daire, had refused to lend it to her in order to best her husband who had a champion bull called Finnbheannach. War ensued and eventually only Cu Cnulainn stood between Meadhbh's army and Ulster. She was defeated, but after a fierce fight the Donn Cuailnge then killed Finnbheannach, before its own heart burst in its breast.

27 Imitation of a Connaught Love Song

This refers to the story of Deirdre and the sons of Usnagh. Deirdre, her lover Naisi and his brothers were in hiding in Scotland from King Connor Mac Nessa. Connor had reared Deirdre from childhood and intended to marry her himself. The sons were unhappy in exile and were easily lured back by Connor who pretended to have forgiven them. However, upon their return he used a druid's spell to freeze them in a sea of ice. When Deirdre found the bodies she lay beside her lover and she too expired.

28 Thoughts at the Trysting Stile

The poem commemorates the poet's courtship of local girl, Ellie Vaughey. Another meeting place was at a large boulder up on the hills. This boulder was transported to the garden of the Ledwidge Cottage Museum, where it can now be viewed.

31 To Lord Dunsany

Addressed to the poet's patron and mentor. Dunsany, a renowned author and big-game hunter offered to take Ledwidge with him to Africa. Frank declined the offer as it would have meant being away from his mother for four months. When Dunsany returned, the poem was printed in the local paper to welcome him home.

32 To Matty McGoona

Matty was the poet's closest friend. He sometimes visited the Ledwidges, but usually Frank cycled to Donaghmore where Matty lived. There, the two would sit on the hop that went under the great chimney breast, or outside in the cherry orchard. Matty often advised Frank and corrected his spelling and grammatical errors. McGoona was a printer by trade, employed by the Irish Peasant and later The Meath Chronicle. The poet learned a lot from him about Irish myths, folklore, nature, astronomy and a variety of subjects. To his dying day, Matty insisted that he had seen Frank's ghost one night while working late at his press in the Meath Chronicle.

33 The Burial of Love

Added to the collection under the title 'The Death of Love.' The original manuscript bearing the above title is contained in the Seumas O'Sullivan papers (Trinity College, Dublin.) Ledwidge, a regular contributor to the Drogheda Independent had not submitted anything for some time and broke a long silence in January, 1914 with this poem, as if to proclaim to the world that his relationship with Ellie Vaughey was over.

34 The Wife of Llew

"Written in a meadow full of flowers and singing birds" -a letter to Prof. Lewis N. Chase. This poem was inspired by an incident related in the 'Mabinogion', a collection of twelfth to fourteenth century Welsh legends. The story is that Llew Llaw Gyffes could not marry a woman of Earthly form, so Gwydion and Math conjured for him a bride made from flowers and birds. Her name was Blodeudd and she was unfaithful.

35 A Song

Here the poet tells us plainly why he thinks the relationship has failed: it is because of the class divide between those with land and those without.

40 Sleep o Grief of Me
Though singled out by Lord Dunsany for publication, this did not appear in any of the original books; presumably because of its controversial theme.

41 The Lost Ones
"Was written in a sad mood when I remembered all whom I knew and who were lost and away forever. I wanted someone to console me by assuring me that beyond this dark they would meet again." - A letter to Lewis N. Chase.

42 The Sister
In this poem the poet may be speaking of his own sister who went to live in Manchester. The child he meets reminds him of her.

44 The Singer's Muse
The muse in this case is clearly his mother. This, and *'My Mother'* are the two main tributes to Mrs. Ann Ledwidge. Here he includes a short epitaph for himself.

45 August
See the reference in the preface. Michael Mc Glynn, musical director of choral group, ANÚNA has produced a beautiful version of this poem set to music. It is to be found on their CD, *'Behind the Closed Eye.'*

46 A Little Boy in the Morning
The poem is dedicated to Jack Tiernan, a local lad who helped out on the neighbouring farms, and who was often seen driving Johnson's cows along the street. Written while Ledwidge was home on leave, at Christmas, Dec. 1914. The boy's untimely death inspired the poem. Prof. Lewis N. Chase of the University of Rochester, New York, compared the poem to Burns' 'Highland Mary,' and used it in a lecture on form. When Ledwidge heard of this he sent a lengthy, autobiographical letter to Lewis from the trenches, which today provides us with much of what we know about him. The letter reached Lewis on 30th June, 1917, a month before the poet's death.

47 The Watcher of the Sea
This poem refers to the story of Bran and Branwyn, the children of Llyr. The story is contained in the Mabinogion. The ancient Celts believed the human head to be the seat of the soul, capable of independent life after the death of the body. They thought it possessed powers of prophecy, symbolized fertility, and provided entertainment in the otherworld. In the myth, Bran is poisoned by an arrow in the foot during a battle with the men of Eireann. He tells his warriors to cut off his head before the poison can reach it; then to bring the severed head to the fortress of Llyr (now London) and to bury it on the White Hill (now the site of the Tower Of London). The head was to be placed facing east to ward off all invaders. As legend has it, so it was until Arthur dug it up and flung it into the sea. Arthur died soon after, leaving the way open to the hoards of invading Angles and Saxons.   This is an important poem in the context that it was written at Richmond Barracks and the poet is stating his reasons for being in the British army.

48 A Prayer
Written at Richmond Barracks, the poem that caused a stir at the Gogarty School: see Preface.

49 To Lizzie
Dedicated to Elizabeth Healy of Slane. Following the break up with Ellie Vaughey, Ledwidge turned his attention to Lizzie. They went to several dances together and shared an interest in books and music. They seemed compatible, but as with Ellie, anything more serious was absolutely out of the question, he being a peasant. Upon joining the army, he bombarded her with love letters from Richmond Barracks. These fortunately have survived, along with the MS of this poem which varies slightly from that published in Songs of Peace.

50 The Call to Ireland
"A very nice lady journalist came to look for information from me yesterday. It seems my poem in the 'Times' (did you see it?) caused a little splash" - a letter to Lizzie Healy, 18th. Feb. 1915.

51 To My Little Nephew Seumas
The nephew was Seumas (more commonly, Seamus) Padraic O'Shanley. Written in April 1915. Ledwidge wrote an earlier version of this poem to Mary Halpin, a little girl who used to bring him tobacco from the village.

55 To One Dead
Written in camp in Basingstoke while he was out walking with his friend and fellow soldier, Robert Christie - The first of many elegies he was to write for Ellie, who died in Manchester on 15th June, 1915, six weeks after child-birth.

56 When Love and Beauty Wander Away
There was a great blizzard in Serbia at the end of November 1915 and hundreds of men went down with frost-bite. Ledwidge wrote to Dunsany; *'...written one awful night of thunder and rain. I was thinking of the end of the world as the Bible predicts it and tried to imagine Love and Beauty leaving the world hand in hand, and we who could not yet die, standing on the edge of a great precipice with no song, no love, no memory'.*

57 The Cobbler of Sari Gueul (Jul)
In March 1916, from his hospital bed in Cairo, Ledwidge wrote to Lord Dunsany and included this poem which he had written earlier. He added the following note explaining the background to the poem; *"Sara Jul is a village in Serbian Macedonia about half way between Lake Doiran and Salonika. Like all Greek villages, Sara Jul is quiet and very beautiful, seen even in the worst conditions of weather as I have seen it. We stood there two days on our retreat, waiting for a train which never came. Sara Jul is like this: one hilly street with the houses built very much out of line. Bread (oh dear me! Bread! What wouldn't we give for a mouthful of bread!) Tins, lanterns, clothes of all colours etc. etc. are displayed in the windows. Quaint signs creak in the wind, and where you see a vine climbing up a house-front underneath you hear my cobblers ham-*

mer". I wonder if people will understand the line: 'Slow steps come fast to the knife and rule.' Of course an old cow walks very slowly and as it gets older it goes slower and therefore faster to the tan-yard".

59 The Departure of Proserpine
Proserpine/a- (Persephone), Daughter of Zeus and Demeter. In Homer's 'Hymn to Demeter', he tells how she was abducted by Hades while picking flowers in the Vale of Nysa. Demeter, goddess of agriculture, was so distraught that she neglected the Earth. A famine soon swept over the land and Zeus intervened, commanding Hades to release Persephone. As Persephone had eaten a pomegranate seed while in the under-world, she could not be completely freed. Hades allowed her to be with her mother for two-thirds of each year and the rest to be spent with him. The story was no doubt meant to account for the barren appearance of Greek fields in summer after harvest before they are invigorated by the autumn rains when the ploughing and sowing begins.

61 The Homecoming of the Sheep
The reality of the situation was so different. While positioned near Sari Gueul, the sol-diers were starving. They became embroiled in a fierce fight with the Bulgars in a bid to secure three sheep. Although they won the skirmish it was not without casualties. *"With our jack-knives we skinned the sheep, and cut off little strips of the hind quar-ters, which we toasted at a fire and ate, half raw... we secured the sheep, and that was all that mattered. We had no more peace in the Balkans after that, and never another dinner."*-Ledwidge, in a war record published (only) in the Sunday Chronicle, 1916.

62 My Mother
Outnumbered by the Bulgars in Serbia, Ledwidge and his company were forced to make a strategic retreat back to Salonika; this meant a march of 90 miles in a constant rainstorm. It was in the course of this march that he collapsed and was taken to hospi-tal in Cairo, where this poem was written. He was shifted from hospital to hospital, five in all, before being transported back to Manchester.

64 Thomas McDonagh
"...the bittern cry" is a direct reference to *'The Yellow Bittern,'* a translation by McDonagh from the Gaelic poet Cathal Buidhe Mac Giolla Ghunna, about a bird that dies of thirst. Ledwidge sent what could be the original draft of his poem to Lily Fogarty, writer and critic with the Irish Review. On arrival at Ebrington Barracks he wrote out the poem an army issue notepaper. This version, with much stronger ending, is the one that is generally known. Dunsany later sent it to Donagh McDonagh, the son of the executed patriot. A story exists that when McDonagh and his men were holding out at Jacobs Factory he sent word to Pearse, then stationed in the G.P.O. The cryptic message read: *"Yellow Bittern."* Pearse understood its meaning: the water ration was running low.

65 Evening Clouds
A tribute to fellow poet of the War, Rupert Brook who died on the Greek Island of Skyros, from blood poisoning due to sunstroke. His contingent was, at the time, prepar-ing to leave for the Dardanelles en route to Gallipoli.

66 Manchester

Ledwidge was moved from the Giza Hospital in Cairo to the Western General Hospital in Manchester. He then went to stay with his married sister, Mary who lived in Manchester. He was there on 4th. May, 1916.

67 Jeu d'Esprit (a witty outburst or sally)

Dedicated to Oliver St. John Gogarty. The original manuscript carries a message 'Don't tell Starkie of this'. This is a reference to Dr. James Sullivan Starkie, otherwise known as Seumas O'Sullivan editor of the Dublin Magazine 1923-1958. Jemmy Quigley, was the County Surveyor for Meath: at a meeting of the Volunteers on 15th. August 1914, Quigley addressed the crowd and lifting his hat said *"Remember boys, it's Ireland first, Ireland last, and (flinging his hat to the ground) Ireland all the time"*. He was arrested after the rising, but released in June 1916. Ashbourne, is a reference to the battle of Ashbourne (28th. April, 1916) where a famous victory was won by fifty men, led by Thomas Ashe, who decisively defeated the RIC and took over four police barracks. Much of Sackville Street was destroyed in the Easter rebellion. When the street was reopened it was renamed O'Connell Street.

68 The Herons

Here the poet remembers Fr. Edward Smyth, curate of Slane 1907-1911, the first one to recognise his talent. Fr. Smyth left Slane to minister in Mountnugent on the shores of Lough Sheelin (in which he was later drowned).

69 The Wedding Morning

Fellow poet, Joseph Mary Plunkett, member of the I.R.B. supreme council and signatory to the 1916 Proclamation, married Grace Gifford, in Kilmainham Gaol on the eve of his execution.

70 The Blackbirds

The Easter Rising, 1916 and the executions that followed had a profound effect on Ledwidge. He lived for only fifteen months after the event, and during that time wrote numerous poems in memory of the men involved.

71 After Court Martial

"One day he had a bit of a night out, and I was too much annoyed to feel very sympathetic about the trouble in which it landed him, for it looked as if he was deliberately harming his own prospects. Being a lance-corporal, and not a private soldier, it landed him in a court-martial; and I said to Major Willock, who was president of the court-martial, "You will go down to posterity as an afflicter of poets." Major Willock was quite distressed, but found no way of avoiding sentencing Ledwidge to lose his lance-corporal's stripe." -From *'Patches Of Sunlight'* - Lord Dunsany. Various reasons are given for Ledwidge's demotion: that he was drunk and disorderly; that he was involved in a row with the Commanding Officer at Richmond Barracks; and that he overstayed his leave. It is reasonable to suppose, as sources indicate, that he lost his stripes a number of times.

76 Old Letters
Although it's difficult to be certain, this would appear to be addressed to Elizabeth Healy. We know that he had ceased communicating with her and that she had apparently moved on. In any event, as with Ellie Vaughey, her family would never have permitted the courtship to blossom.

78 At Currabwee
Currabwee is situated two miles outside Slane on the Drogheda road. The Vardar is a major river of Macedonia /Greece: it rises in the Sar mountains and flows North-N. East turning sharply to flow past Skopje into Greece where it enters the Gulf of Salonika of the Aegean Sea.

84 Soliloquy
The last line: 'Whence honour turns away in shame,' was added to the poem in the 1944 reprint of the original collection. Its omission from previous publications remains a puzzle: was it a printer's error; did another draft of the poem come to light; or, was it not considered politically correct in 1919?

85 Ascension Thursday 1917
One of numerous poems included with letters sent from the Western Front to writer Katherine Tynan.

86 O'Connell Street
Ledwidge arrived back on about the 10th. May 1916, to the devastated city of Dublin. It was then that the full impact of the Easter Rising struck him. His brief visit to O'Connell Street is commemorated in this poem, written a year later in France. He was being political in the very naming of the poem, as the street was at that time known as Sackville Street.

87 The Old Gods
Sent to Katherine Tynan from the Western Front. Is there a note of sarcasm here in the reference to AE's 'little' room? Ledwidge once borrowed £5 from AE and failed to repay it. AE wrote to Lord Dunsany, who immediately reimbursed him and reprimanded Frank. Another draft of the poem reads 'pictured room,' but neither version ever appeared in the original books.

88 To a German Officer
Written at Ypres, July 1917. Ledwidge added a note to say that he wrote this after seeing a wooden cross that his fellow soldiers had erected over the grave of a German Officer. That same month he met his own fate. A working party of soldiers were engaged in repairing the old railway line and road to Pilkem. They were situated at the site known as Le Carrefour des Roses. Due to incessant rain, the men had taken a break and were having some hot tea. A shell exploded beside them. Ledwidge was identified only by his identity disc. The padre, Fr. Devas recorded in his diary, "*Ledwidge killed-blown to bits.*"